Cambridge **Discovery Education**™

▶ **INTERACTIVE READERS**

Series editor: Bob Hastings

LIFE ONLINE
THE DIGITAL AGE

A2+

Kathryn O'Dell

CAMBRIDGE
UNIVERSITY PRESS

University Printing House, Cambridge CB2 8BS, United Kingdom

One Liberty Plaza, 20th Floor, New York, NY 10006, USA

477 Williamstown Road, Port Melbourne, VIC 3207, Australia

314–321, 3rd Floor, Plot 3, Splendor Forum, Jasola District Centre, New Delhi – 110025, India

79 Anson Road, #06–04/06, Singapore 079906

Cambridge University Press is part of the University of Cambridge.

It furthers the University's mission by disseminating knowledge in the pursuit of education, learning and research at the highest international levels of excellence.

www.cambridge.org
Information on this title: www.cambridge.org/9781107650695

© Cambridge University Press 2014

First published 2014
20 19 18 17 16 15 14 13 12 11 10

Printed in Dubai by Oriental Press

A catalogue record for this publication is available from the British Library

Library of Congress Cataloging-in-Publication Data

O'Dell, Kathryn.
  Life online : the digital age / Kathryn O'Dell.
    pages cm. — (Cambridge discovery interactive readers)
  ISBN 978-1-107-65069-5 (pbk. : alk. paper)
1. Electronic information resource searching—uvenile literature. 2. English language—Textbooks for foreign speakers. 3. Readers (Elementary) I. Title.

ZA4060.O44 2013
025.04—dc23

                              2013024757

ISBN 978-1-107-65069-5

Additional resources for this publication at www.cambridge.org

Layout services, art direction, book design, and photo research: Q2ABillSMITH GROUP
Editorial services: Hyphen S.A.
Audio production: CityVox, New York
Video production: Q2ABillSMITH GROUP

Contents

Before You Read:
Get Ready!

We live in a digital world that is changing all the time. There can be dangers, but the digital world also brings people together in interesting ways.

Words to Know

Look at the pictures and read the captions. Then complete the definitions below with the correct highlighted words.

People use smartphones and other electronic devices to communicate with each other.

People share photos and videos on social networking pages.

Files are kept on a computer or on data storage devices.

❶ _____ : talk or write to someone to share information with them

❷ _____ : digital information

❸ _____ : specialized tools

❹ _____ : sharing information with other people using a website

Read the definitions. Then complete the paragraph with the correct highlighted words.

connected: two or more things joined together

mobile: something that you can move

network: a group of computers connected to each other

technology: the use of science to make useful things

trend: something that is changing and becoming popular

You haven't seen them yet, but "wearable computers" might be the next big **1** _____. Devices like computers and phones have been **2** _____ for years. People take them wherever they go. And these devices often work together in a **3** _____. Phones and computers are already **4** _____. Most people have a phone that can go online, too. In the future, people might not just carry **5** _____, they might wear it! People might have phones in their glasses or a watch they can play video games on.

CHAPTER 1

The Birth of the Internet

PEOPLE ALL OVER THE WORLD ARE CONNECTED BY THE INTERNET. HOW DID IT ALL START?

The Information Superhighway, The World Wide Web, The Web, The Net… The Internet has been called many things since it was **created**. But it doesn't matter what it's called, the Internet is a wonderful **invention** that connects people all around the world. It is the key to the digital age. Like the telegraph and the telephone, the Internet heads a long line of inventions that have changed the way people communicate with each other.

Communication Time Line	
1600s	newspapers
1837	electric telegraph
1844	first long-distance telegraph
1876	telephone
1884	first long-distance call
1890s	radio
1914	first international telephone call
1928	television

A telegraph machine

The Internet lets people communicate in many ways – through email, video, and social networking sites, for example. People use the Internet on computers, tablets,[1] and smartphones. But how did the Internet start?

It was partly thanks to a man named J. C. R. Licklider. In 1962, this American scientist had the idea that computers around the world could be connected to each other and share information. After several years of **research**, people working for the US government had a plan for a network called ARPANET. By 1969, four computers were connected to ARPANET.

Digital Communication Time Line	
1943	first large digital computer
1970	Internet
1971	first email is sent
1970s	first commercial[2] computers
1980	first online newspaper
1980s	first commercial cell phones
1986	first commercial email
1990	World Wide Web
1992	first text message is sent
1994	Internet is available to the **public**
2004	Facebook
2007	first successful smartphone

[1] **tablet:** a small, mobile computer
[2] **commercial:** from or about the business world

?

ANALYZE

How do you think the inventions on the time lines helped make the Internet possible?

7

More and more computers were connected to ARPANET, and in 1972, it was shown to the public. The first emails were sent around the same time.

At first, only researchers and the government used computers connected to networks. But the use of the Internet to bring computers into networks was a great idea. And like most good ideas, it quickly **spread**.

By the 1980s, many people had personal computers in their homes, and the World Wide Web, the Internet as we know it today, began in 1990. Now, it is hard to imagine a world that is not connected by the Internet.

Internet Use Around the World	
Country	Millions of people using the Internet in 2012
China	538
The United States	245
Japan	101
Brazil	89
Germany	67
India	137
The United Kingdom	53
France	52
Nigeria	48
Russia	68
South Korea	40
Mexico	42

When the Internet first became available to the public, it was mostly for companies that sold things online. Later, people began using the web to find and share information. With the invention of sites like YouTube and Facebook,

people began using the Internet to communicate with each other in new ways. Now, the Internet is mobile with people using it on smartphones, tablets, and other devices.

Dot What?

Did you ever wonder what the dot and three letters mean at the end of website addresses?

.com = commercial
- started for companies that sold things
- now used for many different kinds of websites

.org = nonprofit organization
- for companies that don't make money

.gov = government
- for US government websites

.edu = education
- for college and university websites

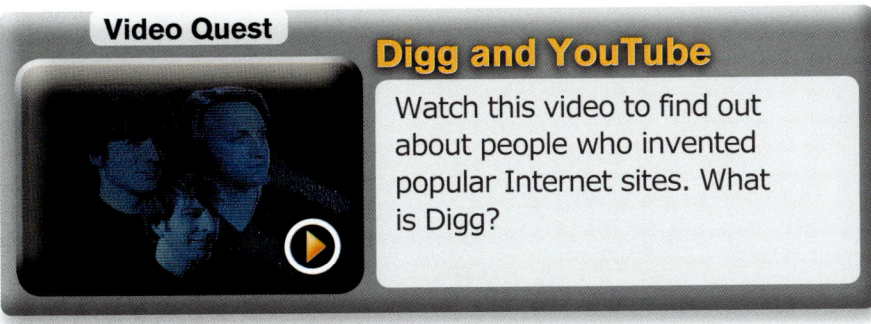

Video Quest

Digg and YouTube

Watch this video to find out about people who invented popular Internet sites. What is Digg?

CHAPTER 2

Liking, Tweeting, Trending

THE INTERNET CONNECTS PEOPLE AROUND THE WORLD. IT ALSO LETS PEOPLE DECIDE WHAT THEY WANT TO READ, SEE, AND SHARE.

Many people use the Internet to reconnect with family and old friends. For example, when Frances Simpson was 18, she started looking for her father. She hadn't seen him since she was three years old. But it wasn't easy. She couldn't find him for a long time.

Then, after looking for 33 years, she finally found him through Facebook. After connecting on the Internet, they talked on the phone, and then they met face-to-face. They hadn't seen each other in almost 50 years.

Social networking is the most popular reason people use the Internet. And Facebook and Twitter are two of the most popular social networking sites.

Most Popular Reasons People Use the Internet	
• Social networking	• Do banking
• Send emails and messages	• Share or look at photos, videos, and files
• Get news and information	
• Get directions to a place	• Play games
• Check the weather	• Look for a job or place to live
• Shop	• Take online classes

Twitter is a site where people post, or put, short personal messages online. These "tweets" can be no more than 140 characters[3] long. It's very popular. In 2012, there were over one billion tweets per day!

Facebook is even more popular. In 2013, there were over 664 million Facebook users. If Facebook were a country, it would have the third largest population[4] in the world after China and India!

Instagram, a photo-sharing site, is also really popular. In January 2013, over 100 million photographs were posted on the site.

[3]**characters:** letters, numbers, and other keyboard symbols
[4]**population:** the number of people living in a place

Video Quest

Facebook

Watch this video to find out about Mark Zuckerberg and Facebook. Where did Facebook start? Who used it?

The Internet has connected people around the world in some unusual ways. In 2012, Korean pop singer Psy posted a video of his song *Gangnam Style* on YouTube. It soon became the most-watched YouTube video of all time with over one billion views.

"Gangnam" song and dance moves started a new web trend. American football player Roy Higgins, some teachers in England, and parents and their babies in Los Angeles have all posted videos doing Psy's dance.

There are even videos with *My Little Pony* cartoons and someone dressed as Gandalf from *Lord of the Rings* doing Psy's moves. Because of the Internet, people around the world are all doing the same dance!

No one knows what the next Internet trend will be and how it will connect people.

Psy (Park Jae-sang) in his *Gangnam Style* video

The Internet connects people in serious[5] ways, too. Many people get news from online news services. Others get more personal news by reading what their friends post about what is going on in the world.

On websites like Digg, readers say what news stories they like, and this helps the website creators decide what kinds of stories to post in the future. People also post photos and videos of things they see, and sometimes they send them to television networks.

People like Mark Zuckerberg, the creator of Facebook, and Jay Adelson, the creator of Digg, think it's good for people to have **control** of what is on the Internet. They think it gives **power** to the people. With the Internet, there is less censorship.[6]

[5]**serious:** important to know about
[6]**censorship:** when governments or companies decide what things can be in books, movies, or news

CHAPTER 3

Online Dangers

THE INTERNET HELPS PEOPLE IN MANY WAYS, BUT THERE ARE ALSO MANY PROBLEMS WITH THE INTERNET.

People having control over Internet **content** can be a good thing, but there are some problems with the Internet. First of all, the information on the Internet is not always true. People can easily post false information.

This can be a problem when people are doing research. In one study, teachers said the Internet helps students do better research. However, the same teachers also said it is difficult for students to find reliable[7] information.

Tips[8] for Finding Reliable Information

- Make sure the website includes the writer's name.
- Look for the date that the information was posted.
- Websites ending in .edu and .org are often reliable.
- Check facts with other websites.

---

[7]**reliable:** something you can be sure is true
[8]**tip:** something useful to know

Another problem is Internet hoaxes.[9] For example, Vera reads online that Mars will be so close to Earth at 4:30 a.m. that it will look like there are two moons in the sky. She sets her alarm and gets up in the middle of the night. But she can only see one moon!

The information she read was a hoax, but false information can spread quickly on social networking sites, and lots of people can think it's true. Another example of a hoax was when someone posted that you can charge your phone with an onion! Don't try it! It isn't true.

Some hoaxes are more dangerous. Some people have lost a lot of money because of emails from fake[10] banks asking them for their banking information.

[9] **hoax:** a plan to make people believe something that is not true
[10] **fake:** not real

Maybe he tried to charge his phone with an onion!

Cyberbullying is another problem on the Internet. Malalia Siafa-Bangura, a New York City student, was cyberbullied on Facebook by a girl from her class at school. The classmate posted mean[11] messages on Malalia's Facebook page and even said she was going to hurt Malalia.

Cyberbullying is a serious problem.

In a 2011 study, 88 percent of American teens that use the Internet said they have seen someone be mean to another person on a social networking site. Cyberbullying can make teens feel terrible, and some even kill themselves. However, in 2012, Malalia decided to do something about it. She wrote a song against cyberbullying, and she sang it with other classmates in an educational program for her school.

Ways to Stop Cyberbullying
• Don't respond.[12]
• Tell a teacher or a parent.
• Save mean messages: you may need to go to the police.
• Tell the police if it doesn't stop.

[11] **mean:** not kind
[12] **respond:** answer

? EVALUATE
What other Internet problems do you know about? Which do you think are the most dangerous?

Betsy Sparrow, a researcher at Columbia University, thinks the Internet changes how we use our brains.

In a study, she looked at Internet usage and memory. People were given 40 facts to type into a computer. Half of the people were told the information was saved, and the others were told it was deleted.[13]

The group that thought the information was deleted remembered more of the facts. Dr. Sparrow says that when we know we can find answers on the Internet, we don't remember as much information.

However, she also found that people remember what websites to go to in order to find different kinds of information better than they remember facts. She doesn't think this is bad, only that the Internet is changing the kinds of things we remember.

[13] **delete:** erase something from a computer

People started listening to music on MP3 players in the late 1990s.

CHAPTER 4

Music and File Sharing

THE INTERNET ALSO CHANGED THE WAY WE BUY AND LISTEN TO MUSIC.

Since the late 1800s, people have recorded music so that others could listen to it. But digital music as we know it today didn't start until the 1980s.

Karlheinz Brandenburg is often called "The Father of the MP3." He started working on a way to record music in small digital files in the 1980s. By the early 1990s, he was ready to change the way we listen to music.

But to use these digital audio files, or sound files, on the Internet he needed a file extension.[14] In July 1995, he chose ".mp3" for the file extension. Brandenburg says that July 14, 1995, is the MP3's birthday.

....

[14] **file extension:** a dot followed by three letters that makes the end of the name of a computer file

With MP3 files, people can listen to music digitally and also share it. In 1999, Shawn Fanning started Napster, a website that let people share MP3 files.

The band Metallica took Shawn Fanning and Napster users to court in 2000.

The creation of Napster changed the world of buying and selling music. For the first time, people could download songs free instead of buying them.

The people in the music business said that Shawn Fanning and people using Napster were breaking the law.[15] The record companies and music artists were angry because they were losing money. The band Metallica took Fanning and 300,000 Napster users to court. They said that they were stealing their music. Then the record companies took Fanning to court, too.

In 2001, Napster shut down.

[15] **law:** what a government says people have to do
[16] **community:** a group of people who do things together

Video Quest

Napster

Watch this video to find out about Shawn Fanning and Napster. How did Napster create a web community?[16]

Howard King, one of Metallica's lawyers, said that file sharing was "not only potentially[17] the end of the music business, but the end of the movie business, the end of the book business, and really the end of protection for intellectual property."[18] After Napster, other sites, like YouTube, started sharing music files and videos.

New laws were made to **protect** musicians and the music business. But the story of Napster gave Steve Jobs, the owner of Apple, an idea. He wanted to create a way for people to buy songs online without breaking the law and a way for musicians to get money for their songs. So, he started an online music store that he called iTunes. By 2012, about 435 million people were buying music on iTunes.

iTunes is a popular online music player and store.

[17] **potentially:** possibly

[18] **intellectual property:** someone's idea, invention, or creation that is protected by law

ANALYZE

Do you think Howard King was right when he said Napster was the end of the music, movie, and book business? Why or why not?

Musicians use the Internet to promote their music.

Today, not so many musicians are worried about people stealing their music. iTunes and other ways of selling music online help them make money. And now, there are laws to protect their intellectual property. Studies show that fewer than 30 percent of artists feel that file sharing is a problem. In fact, most musicians use the Internet to promote[19] their music online. Many musicians also offer free music online. They say this helps them sell more songs and concert tickets.

Every year, there are more and more movies, songs, and books available online. So the fight for artists to protect their intellectual property isn't going to end any time soon. However, for musicians and other artists, there are both advantages[20] and disadvantages in the digital world.

....

[19] **promote:** advertise something
[20] **advantage:** something that helps you

CHAPTER 5

What Do You Think?

TECHNOLOGY IS CHANGING THE WAY WE CONNECT DIGITALLY.

What does our digital future look like?

Many people say that one day soon all our music, movies, art, books, and newspapers will only be in digital form. Will people only use e-readers in their regular lives and go to museums to see real paper books? Will people only take classes from home and never enter a classroom? Will they only watch movies online? Will movie theaters be a thing of the past? Will people stop using paints and only create digital art?

Doing It Online

- In 2012, for the first time, Amazon.com sold more e-books than print books.
- In 2009, 5.6 million people took at least one online college class.
- Americans bought 50 million fewer movie tickets in 2012 than in 2011.

Communication has changed a lot from the invention of the telegraph in 1837 to the Internet as we know it today. How will we communicate 180 years from now? The way we used the Internet in the past was called Web 1.0. The way we use it today – in which everyday users can control the content – is called Web 2.0. Will there be a Web 3.0? What will it look like?

Some think people in the future won't have good relationships[21] with other people because they will only know how to communicate online. Many think we will use new technology to communicate from our brains to computers without using a keyboard or a mouse. But others think the digital age will come to an end, and we will go back to the way things were before the Internet.

[21] **relationship:** the way two people are connected

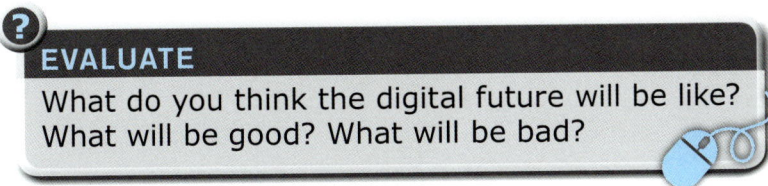

? EVALUATE

What do you think the digital future will be like? What will be good? What will be bad?

Technology can help us communicate in many new ways.

Apple Siri: On an iPhone with Siri, you can tell your phone to send messages, make phone calls, and find directions. Siri asks you questions, too, to find out what you want to do on your phone.

Dragon Dictate: With Dragon Dictate, you talk, and your computer types what you say. It is five times faster than typing.

NextWindow: NextWindow lets you create art using your fingers or brushes on a computer screen.

Emotiv EPOC: This is a headset you wear. With it, you can create music and art just by thinking. You can also play computer games with your brain. People who cannot move their arms can use it to control their wheelchair with their mind.

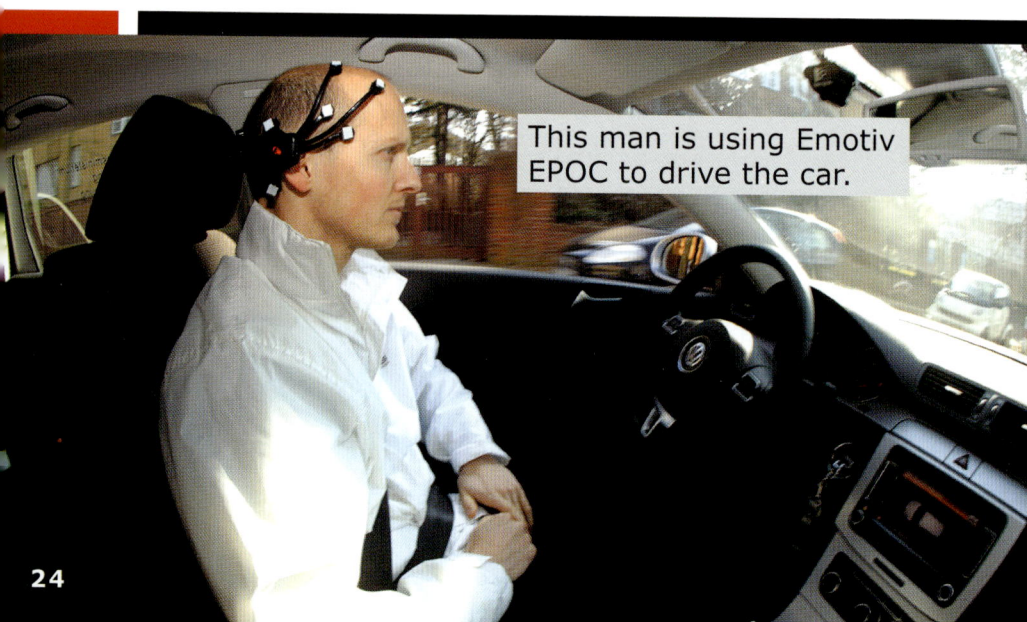

This man is using Emotiv EPOC to drive the car.

Power Translator: This is a program that translates letters, emails, and websites from one language to another.

P300 Speller: People are working on this brain-to-computer program. A person wears a hat that reads signals[22] in the brain. The computer types what the person is thinking.

Kinect for Xbox 360: With Kinect, you can control video games by moving your body.

You can control a computer with your body in some video games.

Do you use any of this technology? Who do you think it's useful for? What are the advantages of this technology? What are the disadvantages?

How do you think people will use voice control, controlling a computer with the body, and brain-to-computer technology in the future?

[22]**signal:** a sound, light, or other thing that gives information

After You Read

Choose the Correct Answers

Circle all of the answers that are correct for each item.

1 What is another word for the Internet?
- Ⓐ The Information Superhighway
- Ⓑ The World Wide Web
- Ⓒ The Cyber Network
- Ⓓ The Net

2 Which people were leaders of the web as we know it today?
- Ⓐ Chad Hurley
- Ⓑ Jay Adelson
- Ⓒ Kevin Rose
- Ⓓ Howard King

3 What are some Internet problems?
- Ⓐ Cyberbullying
- Ⓑ Remembering websites to find information
- Ⓒ Getting false information online
- Ⓓ Hoaxes

4 Who had something to do with Napster?
- Ⓐ Chad Hurley
- Ⓑ Mark Zuckerberg
- Ⓒ Shawn Fanning
- Ⓓ The band Metallica

5 Which facts are true?
- Ⓐ Fewer Americans go to movie theaters than they did in the past.
- Ⓑ Most artists only paint digitally today.
- Ⓒ Millions of people take classes online.
- Ⓓ No one buys print books today.

Complete the Sentences

Use the words in the box to complete the sentences.

ARPANET   brains   cyberbullying   digital   social networking

1 _____ was the first computer network.

2 _____ is the most popular reason to use the Internet.

3 _____ is when people post mean messages online.

4 Researchers say the Internet changes the way we use our _____ .

5 Someday, we might only read _____ newspapers.

Complete the Text

Use the words in the box to complete the text.

communicate   mobile devices   social networking   technology   trend

As of 2012, Nigeria had 48 million Internet users. It has the most Internet users of any country in Africa. Nigerians use the Internet at home, but they also use it on **1** _____ .
Over 80 million Nigerians have cell phones, and it is a growing **2** _____ to use phones to connect to the Internet. In fact, most Nigerians between the ages of 18 and 27 use their phones more than they use computers.

They also love **3** _____ sites like Facebook. **4** _____ has helped people in Nigeria **5** _____ with each other.

Your Opinion

What do you think is the most important invention in the digital age? Why?

Answer Key

Words to Know, page 4

1 communicate **2** files **3** devices **4** social networking

Words to Know, page 5

1 trend **2** mobile **3** network **4** connected **5** technology

Analyze, page 7 *Answers will vary.*

Video Quest, page 9
Digg is a social news site. Everyday people choose the content.

Video Quest, page 11
Facebook started at Harvard University. After that, students at all of the colleges in the USA started using it.

Evaluate, page 16 *Answers will vary.*

Video Quest, page 19
It became a community because people shared music, and they started communicating about music online.

Analyze, page 20 *Answers will vary.*

Evaluate, page 23 *Answers will vary.*

Choose the Correct Answers, page 26

1 a, b, d **2** a, b, c **3** a, c, d **4** c, d **5** a, c

Complete the Sentences, page 27

1 ARPANET **2** Social networking **3** Cyberbullying **4** brains **5** digital

Complete the Text, page 27

1 mobile devices **2** trend **3** social networking **4** Technology **5** communicate

Your Opinion, Page 27 *Answers will vary.*